AF131397

BOOK ANALYSIS

By Benjamin Taylor

A Tale of Two Cities

BY CHARLES DICKENS

Bright
≡Summaries.com

CHARLES DICKENS

ENGLISH NOVELIST AND SHORT STORY WRITER

- **Born in Portsmouth in 1812.**
- **Died near Chatham in 1870.**
- **Notable works:**
  - *A Christmas Carol* (1843), novella
  - *David Copperfield* (1850), novel
  - *Great Expectations* (1861), novel

Charles Dickens was an English novelist who is considered to be the greatest writer of the Victorian era, to the point that many of his novels and the characters in them are synonymous with readers' conceptualisation of the period. He was born in Portsmouth in 1812 to a middle-class family before moving to London in 1820 – the city where he would live for much of his life. In 1824, when financial ruin caused his father to be sent to debtors' prison, he was forced to drop out of school and work in a factory. This period of his childhood was said to influence much of his later life and work. After working as a clerk and a newspaper reporter, Dickens began his literary career with the serialised novel *The Pickwick Papers* (1837) and went on to publish 15 novels, five novellas and numerous short stories. He achieved extreme popularity during his lifetime and widespread critical praise ever since, with many of his characters becoming English literary icons. Beyond the hundreds of adaptations of his books for film, television and the stage, Dickens' work is remembered for its comic wit, vivid characterisation and social criticism.

A TALE OF TWO CITIES

THE GREAT WAVE OF REVOLUTION

- **Genre:** novel
- **Reference edition:** Dickens, C. (1999) *A Tale of Two Cities*. Ware: Wordsworth Editions Limited.
- **1ˢᵗ edition:** 1859
- **Themes:** revolution, society, law, justice, class, poverty, nature, love, history, France

Published in 1859, towards the end of his life, *A Tale of Two Cities* is Charles Dickens' second and most famous historical novel. The novel, which is split into three books, spans a period of several years and explores the social and cultural conditions in the run-up to and duration of the French Revolution (1775-99). The first book is set in 1775 and the last in 1792, and the novel as a whole follows a group of characters in London and Paris through the great event of the century. The novel was published serially and as a book, with much of the historical context purportedly taken from Thomas Carlyle's *The French Revolution: A*

History (1837). It was wildly popular on release and has become one of Dickens' most famous and well-loved novels, with a large number of stage, film and television adaptations appearing over the years, including Jack Conway's 1935 film. Though, like much of Dickens' work, the novel is critically celebrated, the historical validity of his account of the French Revolution and the events surrounding it has often been called into question.

SUMMARY

BOOK ONE - RECALLED TO LIFE

In 1775, Mr Jarvis Lorry, a manager at Tellson's Bank in London, is on his way to Dover when he receives a message relating to the reappearance of an old acquaintance, a Dr Manette, who has been released from the Bastille in France after 18 long years of imprisonment. Lorry meets with Manette's daughter, Lucie, and the two travel to Paris together. Dr Manette is lodging with Mr and Mrs Defarge, the owners of a wine shop in Paris. His time in prison has made him a ghost of the man he once was, with much of his personality replaced by a traumatic obsessive hobby for shoemaking. As such, he does not recognise Mr Lorry and only just recognises his daughter by her hair and its resemblance to her mother's.

BOOK TWO - THE GOLDEN THREAD

Five years later, Jerry Cruncher, an odd-jobs man in London, is summoned to the Old Bailey as a messenger for Mr Lorry. He finds on his arrival the trial of

Sir Charles Darnay, an acquaintance of Lorry, Dr Manette and Lucie from the voyage back to England, who is accused of treason and almost certain to die for giving away British secrets about troops in North America. He is acquitted, however, when his lawyers Mr Stryver and Mr Carton discredit the testimony against him by drawing a physical comparison between the accused and Carton himself.

Back in France, on the way back from a party, a French noble named Marquis St Evrémonde, who in his cruelty and disdain for those in po-verty represents what we imagine of the French aristocracy at the time, runs over and kills a child in his carriage. The Marquis shows no regret and instead hurls a gold coin at the grieving father, and another at Mr Defarge, in whose town the murder took place. Later that night, the Marquis is visited by none other than Charles Darnay, who as it turns out is his nephew and sole heir. Charles is pained by the French aristocratic sys-tem of which he is a part and renounces both his family name and his inheritance to the contempt of his uncle, wishing instead to pursue his career and relationships in England. The next morning the Marquis is found murdered in his bed.

In London some time later, Charles Darnay, now established as a French tutor, goes to see Dr Manette in the hope of securing his blessing to marry Lucie. Manette is saddened at the prospect of losing her but promises not to stand in his way. Little do they know that across at Tellson's, Mr Stryver is asking Lorry about his own suitability for Lucie, though Lorry attempts to persuade him against it. Mr Carton, who is renowned for a personal life of debauchery and drunkenness, is also in love with Lucie and confesses it to her along with his many miseries, making her promise not to tell anyone. In Paris, a spy turns up at the wine shop owned by the Defarges hoping for information concerning revolutionary sentiment. Madame Defarge knits all the way through, and it is revealed that she knits in code the names of people who are to be killed during the Revolution.

In England, Charles Darnay marries Lucie in a private ceremony. Her father appears contented throughout – though once they leave for their honeymoon, he retreats back into a reflection of the trauma of his imprisonment, returning to his shoemaking for nine days straight. He snaps out of it, however, and Mr Lorry destroys the shoemaking implements. Several years pass and the couple have children, keeping Lorry, Stryver and Carton as firm family friends while worrying news from France trickles through.

In Paris tension continues to rise, and Madame Defarge and her husband take part in the Storming of the Bastille, releasing prisoners and brutally killing officers. The year is now 1789, and we hear tales of various aristocrats being cap-tured and killed and their estates burned to the ground. French aristocrats begin streaming out of France, taking their money with them. One day, Mr Lorry decides that he must go to Paris, despite it being in the throes of violent revolu-tion, in order to secure important documents from the Parisian branch of Tellson's. Charles Darnay is unnerved by the French situation. He feels guilty because of his heritage and is convinced of secretly travelling to Paris when he receives a letter from an imprisoned servant of his murdered uncle imploring him to somehow administer his release.

BOOK THREE – THE TRACK OF A STORM

On arriving in France, Charles is instantly arrested for his status as an emigrant and put in a prison called La Force without charge or trial as the Revolution becomes ever more violent. Mr Lorry is shocked when Lucie, her father and Miss Pross turn up at the bank in Paris and tell him the news. Dr Manette attempts to use his influence as a former Bastille prisoner to get Charles out and manages to be appointed the acting physician for three prisons, including La Force. After much preparation, when Charles' trial comes up it goes well, and with the help of Dr Manette he is released. Later that night, however, Charles is taken prisoner again, having been accused by none other than the Defarges.

Mr Carton arrives in Paris just as Miss Pross bumps into her long-lost brother, who is working as a spy for the Republic under the name Barsad. Carton threatens to reveal his true identity unless he helps him in his plans to get Charles released. At the trial the next day, however, things go awry for Charles, as a letter found by Defarge in Dr Manette's cell in the Bastille from years ago is used as evidence against him. The letter details how Manette was imprisoned by the Evrémonde brothers (Charles' father and uncle), who one night summoned him to try to save the life of a young peasant girl and her brother. Charles' uncle had raped the girl and stabbed her brother, and Dr Manette was sent to the Bastille for refusing to keep quiet about the horrible crimes. He ends the letter by denouncing the brothers and their descendants, which the court takes as enough reason to sentence Charles to death by guillotine.

After the trial Mr Carton overhears that Madame Defarge is the sister of the raped woman and slain man in Manette's letter and that she wants to have the entire family, including Lucie and her child, killed as well. After hearing this, Carton returns to the house and tells Mr Lorry that they must leave France immediately. He then goes to see Charles at the prison, tricks him into swapping clothes with him and drugs him, taking his place as the prisoner. Barsad is on hand to take Charles to safety, while Carton is taken to be executed.

Meanwhile, Lucie, Manette and Lorry having left in a rush, Miss Pross and Jerry Cruncher wait at the house making the last of the arrangements. Madame Defarge arrives heavily armed, however, and demands to see Lucie in the hope of incriminating her. Miss Pross refuses her entry and the two tussle, with the fight ending in Madame Defarge being shot dead and Miss Pross going deaf.

The book ends with Carton's thoughts in the run-up to his execution.

CHARACTERS

JARVIS LORRY

Jarvis Lorry is the character with whom *A Tale of Two Cities* begins. He is a manager at Tellson's Bank in London and an old friend of the newly released Dr Manette. Throughout the novel, Mr Lorry is defined by both his preoccupation with business and his deep affection for Lucie and her husband and father – a duality of personality which seems to be in conflict at times. We are told that his face: "habitually supressed and quieted, was still lighted up under the quaint wig by a pair of moist bright eyes that must have cost their owner, in years gone by, some pains to drill to the composed and reserved expression of Tellson's Bank" (p. 15). He seems to play up to this character trope in the novel, constantly claiming to be a man of business, to have "no feelings, and that all the relations I hold with my fellow-creatures are mere business relations" (p. 20). He is, however, devoted to his friends, going to great lengths to retrieve Dr Manette from Paris and care for him and his family through the various difficulties they encounter.

He begins the book in his sixties and is well into his eighties by its conclusion. He never marries and is described by Miss Pross at one point as being "a bachelor in [his] cradle" (p. 164), so suited is he to the world of business and singledom.

DR MANETTE

At the start of the novel, Dr Manette, a native Frenchman, has just recently been freed after 18 years of unjust incarceration in the Bastille, a famous fortress used for centuries as a prison by the French state. Due to the isolation and spiritual devastation of such a long imprisonment, Dr Manette is a wreck of a man, with "a white beard, raggedly cut, but not very long, a hollow face, and exceedingly bright eyes." (p. 34). His voice is compared to "a once beautiful colour faded away into a poor weak stain" (p. 33), a comparison which indeed reflects the effect of his trauma on the entirety of his being. Dr Manette's mental anguish is represented in his compulsive shoemaking, a vocation which he took up during his imprisonment, and which he returns to at moments throughout the novel when the memory of his ordeal overshadows his newly recovered personality.

Dr Manette is only saved from the madness of his compulsion – which reduces his whole person to one single activity – by his daughter, Lucie, whose resemblance to her mother shocks him out of his nightmare: "only his daughter had the power of charming this black, brooding from his mind. She was the golden thread that united him to a Past beyond his misery" (p. 66). Due to his periodic lapses into despondency, we can never be sure that the Doctor is freed from the tragedy of his past, despite the relative joy of his present. However, he finds in revolutionary France, where his long and unjust imprisonment is treated with respect and notoriety, that his spirit has not been wholly crushed when "for the first time the Doctor felt, now, that his suffering gave him strength and power" (p. 232).

LUCIE MANETTE

Lucie, who was born in France but carried to England by Mr Lorry after her father's imprisonment, is 17 years old at the start of the novel, "a short, slight, pretty figure, a quantity of golden hair, a pair of blue eyes that met his own with an inquiring look" (p. 18). One of her first acts in the novel involves her rousing her father, who she had assumed dead, from his reverie seemingly by the sheer force of her love for him: "trembling with eagerness to lay the spectral face upon her warm young breast and love it back to life" (p. 36). She acts similarly throughout the book and at times resembles an idealised version of English feminine gentility, defined by her care for others, her devotion to her father (Dr Manette) and husband (Charles Darnay), a picture of "earnest youth and beauty" (p. 58).

She is the object of the desires of three separate characters in the novel, though out of Mr Carton, Mr Stryver and Charles Darnay, she chooses Charles, who she has a daughter with and who, if her desperate actions in the final third of the book are anything to go by, she is very much in love with.

MADAME DEFARGE

Madame Therese Defarge lives in Paris and helps run a wine shop with her husband, Ernest. She is also an intrinsic and increasingly dominant component of the revolutionary movement in France, helping plan and direct the growing discontent of the French people and taking a prominent position once violence ensues, notably pictured with the Governor's body "down on the sole of the shoe of Madame Defarge where she had trodden on the body to steady it for mutilation" (p. 188). Madame Defarge is representative of the often-conflicting righteousness and frenzy of revolution. We find out late in the novel that her whole family was decimated by the actions of the Marquis St Evrémonde, and as such she is so focussed on vengeance that she is defined by it in her every action, from her endless knitting of the names of those to be killed to random domestic chores: "she tied a knot with flashing eyes, as if it throttled a foe" (p. 152). Though she abides through much of the plot as a heroic figure, and is indeed often praised heavily by those around her for her bravery and power, Madame Defarge increasingly comes to represent a revolution that is spiralling beyond the bounds of justice – something which Dickens attempts to explain: "imbued from her childhood with a brooding sense of wrong, and an inveterate hatred of a class, opportunity had developed her into a tigress" (p. 309).

CHARLES DARNAY

Charles Darnay is yet another French-born man living in England who we first encounter being tried for treason in London. He is proved innocent with the help of Mr Lorry, Dr Manette, and Lucie – who he becomes deeply infatuated with and eventually marries. He is described as "a young man of about five-and-twenty, well-grown and well-looking, with a sunburnt cheek and a dark eye. His condition was that of a young gentleman" (p. 51). Charles is furthermore the nephew and heir of the Marquis St Evrémonde, a French aristocrat who is murdered towards the start of the book. He is guilt-ridden at his place in such an unequal society, however: "bound to a system that is frightful to me, responsible for it, but powerless in it" (p. 105), and renounces his name and inheritance, choosing instead to work and find his place in England. It is this guilt which brings him back to France in the hope of saving the life of one of his uncle's old servants, and it is here that he is captured and sentenced to death as a result of his aristocratic heritage. He is only saved by the sacrificial kindness of Mr Carton, whose physical resemblance to Charles gives him the opportunity to die in his place.

ANALYSIS

HISTORICAL CONTEXT

A Tale of Two Cities spans almost two decades (1775-92) of intense social change in Europe and around the world, and as a historical novel uses its central plot and characters to explore the historical and social conditions surrounding the French Revolution. The French Revolution is renowned for being one of the most important events in modern human history, encompassing the abolition of the French monarchy and regicide of King Louis XVI and the establishment of a democratic republic. The events of the Revolution took place between 1787 and 1799 but climaxed in what is known as the Revolution of 1789. Its causes are varied but include a general dissatisfaction with the outdated feudal system and the economic bankruptcy of France as a result of costly endeavours such as the American War of Independence (1775-1783) and the Seven Years War (1756-1763) which, combined with a string of bad harvests, exacerbated already dreadful living conditions and high taxation for the burgeoning peasant population. Dickens explores these social conditions, and reasons behind the Revolution throughout the novel, including examples of pre-revolutionary inter-class belligerence and the unjust and twisted nature of France's ancient institutions. *A Tale of Two Cities* furthermore depicts certain key events in the French Revolution, including the Storming of the Bastille in July 1789.

Much of the novel also takes place in London, during the reign of King George III, who held the throne of Great Britain from 1760 to 1820. During the period explored in the book, Britain was at war with both America and France, winning the Seven Years War but losing its American colonies. Patriotic distrust of both enemies can be seen in *A Tale of Two Cities*: for example, at the start of the novel, the French Charles Darnay is being tried for treason against Britain for purportedly giving information about troops to the Americans, and is condemned for saying: "perhaps George Washington might gain almost as great a name in history as George the Third" (p. 60).

SOCIAL CONDITIONS IN FRANCE

One of the major intentions of Dickens' work more generally – the exploration of the social conditions of the poor – is also present in *The Tale of Two Cities*, as he reveals the historical exploitation and mistreatment of the French peasants around which a portion of the plot revolves. This exploration also has the benefit of revealing a major contributing factor to the events of the French Revolution. We are shown early in the novel the drastic levels of inequality between the richest and poorest sections of French society, with the narrator saying of the section of Paris he focusses on: "the children had ancient faces and grave voices; and upon them, and upon the grown faces, and ploughed into every furrow of age and coming up fresh, was the sign, Hunger" (p. 25). This is contrasted with the sickening extravagance of the Marquis St Evrémonde, the aristocrat who needs four servants to serve him his chocolate: "It took four men, all four a-blaze with gorgeous decoration, and the Chief of them unable to exist with fewer than two gold watches in his pocket, emulative of the noble and chaste fashion set by Monsieur to conduct the happy chocolate to Monseigneur's lips" (p. 88).

One scene in particular illustrates the alarming difference between the two social classes, when the Marquis runs over a baby in his carriage. Defarge comforts the father of the child, saying "It has died in a moment without pain. Could it have lived an hour as happily?" (p. 94) as the Marquis looks on the crowd "as if they had been mere rats come out of their holes" (*ibid.*). Such severe social conditions make clear the reasons for the revolution of a working class so poor and taxed by the government that death is more palatable than the prolonged suffering of life.

Comparisons of social conditions can of course be made with Britain – and in particular the lives of the working poor in industrial London so famously explored by Dickens himself. Indeed, the events of the book and the violence of the retaliation of the revolutionaries can be seen as a warning to Dickens' British contemporaries about the consequences of the exploitative, unjust and cruel treatment of the poorest in society. In the final chapter of the novel, this warning is set out clearly: "Crush humanity out of shape once more, under similar hammers, and it will twist itself into the same tortured forms. Sow the same seed of rapacious licence and oppression over again, and It will surely yield the same fruit according to its kind" (p. 316).

THE REVOLUTION AS ELEMENTAL

In tandem with his descriptions of the movements of the French revolutionaries, Dickens employs natural and elemental imagery, particularly in descriptions of the mob to convey the sublime and primal nature of its retribution. One of the recurring images is that of the sea, with the crowd described as "the living sea" which "rose, wave on wave, depth on depth and overflowed the city" (p. 183), rising and falling in unison. Further examples of this kind of imagery can be found in the conversations between Madame Defarge and her husband while she attempts to stoke the fires of proletarian anger. She compares revolution to an earthquake, for example claiming that "it does not take a long time [...] for an earthquake to swallow a town. Eh well! Tell me how long it takes to prepare the earthquake" (p. 152). Another example can be seen when Dickens describes the crowd as "a forest of naked arms struggl[ing] in the air like shrivelled branches of trees in a winter wind" (p. 182). In each example, the revolutionary horde is described as a natural force that is chaotic, all-powerful and above all unstoppable, representing the power of collective human action and equating the French Revolution to something like the will of nature.

These various images also tend to frame the Revolution as something that is inevitable due to the cyclical permanence of the movements of the natural world. As such, we are again reminded of the inevitability of revolution in light of the social conditions present in France and warned that the same natural explosion of humanity might make its way across the Channel: "perhaps, see that great crowd of people with its rush and roar, bearing down upon them, too" (p. 87).

JUSTICE

Another central theme in *A Tale of Two Cities* is that of justice, and what justice means to the different people in the book. This theme is particularly prominent due to the nature of the French Revolution, which involves the redefinition of the rule of law; the discarding of the old, unfair rules for the new. The French people have of course been treated unfairly, in a social structure which exploits and harms them. After the Revolution, however, Dickens presents a society in which the traditional rule of law has been replaced by a vacuum, in which the various whims of the people are considered justice and large, often disinterested crowds decide the fates of prisoners on impulse. Dickens shows how large numbers of innocent people are caught up in the incrimination of an entire social class, and as we see the vague and vicious retaliation of a wronged people, we come to question what the idea of justice means in the novel. This can be seen when Charles is sent to prison on his arrival in France. When he protests his innocence, he is told by Defarge: "Other people have been similarly buried in worse positions, before now" (p. 216). Is it right for Charles, an innocent man, to suffer as the victims of his uncle suffered?

The issue of justice is further explored in the character of Madame Defarge, who almost obsessively goes about trying to right the wrongs of her past and avenge her dead family by eliminating the entire lineage of their oppressors. We can clearly see, however, that her proposed murder of not only Charles, but also Lucie and their daughter, does not constitute justice and would seem maniacal but for Dickens explanation: "it was nothing to her, that an innocent man was to die for the sins of his forefathers; she saw, not him, but them" (p. 309). As such, justice in *A Tale of Two Cities* is not always the same and we come to see two versions of it in the novel: that which is individual and emotional and that which is dictated by the court, represented in the moniker above the Old Bailey in London of "whatever is is right" (p. 50).

FURTHER REFLECTION

SOME QUESTIONS TO THINK ABOUT...

- Do you think that Dickens sacrifices historical accuracy for dramatic power? Is it right for him to do so?
- How do Madame Defarge and Charles Darnay's ideas of justice differ? Considering the cruel and exploitative nature of French aristocrats like Charles' uncle, is there any validity in his imprisonment?
- Dickens has been accused of having flat, one-dimensional characters. Consider characters like the Marquis St Evrémonde and Madame Defarge. Are these characters well rounded? Explain your answer.
- In reflection of this, does Dickens do justice to the character of Lucie? How is she portrayed in the novel?
- Do you think that Dickens takes sides when describing the French Revolution? Does he sympathise with the prisoners more than the revolutionaries?

- What comparisons can we make between the social conditions of this period of France and those in Victorian England?
- Do you think that the French aristocracy is portrayed accurately? Is the Marquis St Evrémonde a caricature of evil and snobbery?
- Given the complex and wide-ranging nature of the plot and its settings, think about how you might go about directing a film or stage adaptation of *A Tale of Two Cities*. Would the novel work in either form? Why/why not?

We want to hear from you!
Leave a comment on your online library
and share your favourite books on social media!

FURTHER READING

REFERENCE EDITION

- Dickens, C. (1999) *A Tale of Two Cities*. Ware: Wordsworth Editions Limited.

ADAPTATIONS

- *A Tale of Two Cities*. (1935) [Film]. Jack Conway. Dir. US: MGM.

MORE FROM BRIGHTSUMMARIES.COM

- Reading guide – *A Christmas Carol* by Charles Dickens.

- Reading guide – *Bleak House* by Charles Dickens.

- Reading guide – *David Copperfield* by Charles Dickens.

- Reading guide – *Great Expectations* by Charles Dickens.

- Reading guide – *Hard Times* by Charles Dickens.

- Reading guide – *Oliver Twist* by Charles Dickens.

www.brightsummaries.com

Ebook EAN: 9782808018715

Paperback EAN: 9782808018722

Legal Deposit: D/2019/12603/102

Cover: © Primento

Digital conception by Primento, the digital partner of publishers.